One Last Act

One Last Act:

A Mental Health Clinician's Guide to Professional Wills

Cathy Wilson, LPC, ACS

ISBN: 978-1-7345714-1-7

Book cover and interior by alittlefeather.com

onelastact.net

Praise for One Last Act

"Licensed Professional Counselor Cathy Wilson's book, One Last Act: A Mental Health Clinician's Guide to Professional Wills, fills a significant gap in the professional literature and ethical mandates by providing clinical guidance and ethical planning for therapists in completing that one last act that permits continuity of care for mental health clients.

In One Last Act, mental health professionals finally have a practical, values-based, culturally sensitive guide and simple-to-use guide for taking care of clients' needs when faced with unexpected interruptions and terminations due to a clinician's incapacities and physical death.

By providing exercises and examples throughout the book, Wilson walks us through the surprisingly simple steps and reflection necessary to ultimately complete a therapist's professional will.

This easy-to-follow guide covers why we need such a document, how to choose a professional executor (and why you might choose to be one), why a one-size-fits-all document will not suffice, who needs to be contacted (when and how), the additional information that may be needed to carry out a clinician's wishes, and how / where to store the completed professional will."

Tamara G. Suttle, MEd, LPC, ACS
Founder of Private Practice From the Inside Out

"Cathy Wilson has created a down-to-earth, must-read handbook for creating a professional will. This book is filled with important information for counselors-in-training, practitioners thinking about starting a private practice, and experienced clinicians who are dragging their feet."

Jude T. Austin II, Ph.D., LPC, LMFT-Associate, NCC, CCMHC
Assistant Professor at University of Mary Hardin-Baylor
Julius A. Austin, Ph.D., PLPC
Clinical Therapist and Coordinator of the Office of Substance Abuse and Recovery at Tulane University
Authors of *Surviving and Thriving in Your Counseling Program*

"A much-needed resource to help mental health professionals, leaders, and supervisors feel prepared for the unexpected! This book and it's tools are a great way to reduce anxiety and embrace planning that supports both our clients and the businesses we've worked so hard to create!"

Khara Croswaite Brindle, LPC
Founder of Croswaite Counseling and co-author of *The Empowerment Model of Clinical Supervision: A roadmap through the complexities of community mental health*

"This breakthrough book, "One Last Act: A Mental Health Clinician's Guide to Professional Wills" is well researched, written in a clear and understandable fashion, and replete with valuable information for any mental health practitioner looking create a Professional Will.

The author has included a Professional Will template for mental health providers to follow in order to effectively create their own Professional Will. Creation of a Professional Will is not only a legal obligation but an ethical one as well for the protection of clients and their loved ones.

This book should be on every mental health provider's bookshelf and it should be closely followed to create a working Professional Will in an attempt to Do No Harm to our clients.

I highly recommend this book and the Professional Will template for all Mental Health Providers. Ms. Wilson has created an extremely valuable resource and in doing so has helped the mental health profession address a difficult but invaluable topic."

John Arman, Ph.D., LPC
Professor and Clinical Supervisor in the Regis University Counseling Graduate Program, Denver, Colorado

"A great resource for mental health and other health care professionals."

John R. Edwards, LCSW
West Coast Psychotherapy, Oakland, CA

Acknowledgements

I am grateful to work with many talented colleagues in the mental health field. To the clinicians who have attended my workshops, those I meet with for consultation - both one-on-one and in our consultation groups, the staff at LifePaths, and those I have met virtually via phone, email and social media: thank you, I wouldn't have been able to accomplish this without your support. Your friendship, collaboration, support, and ability to tolerate my quirks and flaws are worth more to me than words can ever say.

In particular, thank you to Tamara Suttle for your "nudges," your coaching, your no-nonsense ethics, and the never-ending laughter we share every time we are together. Anyone who is able to have you as their coach or counselor is very fortunate.

Thanks to Alicia Hutchens with A Little Feather for your knowledge and support in putting this book together. Your support has been amazing!

Thanks also to Julie for providing such a beautifully written and helpful Foreword for this book. Your support has also been amazing!

And finally, thanks to my son and daughter, Andrea and Logan, for not only putting up with listening to me talk (a lot) about professional wills and this book, but for being great people in my life. I love you a lot and I'm so glad I'm the one who got to be your mom.

Table of Contents

Disclaimer

The contents of this book are not intended in any way as legal advice. The author is not an attorney and cannot speak to specific circumstances a mental health clinician may have. The information in this book should not be used as a substitute for formal consultation on legal or ethical issues, and you should consider such formal consultation prior to making decisions regarding your individual circumstances. Where possible, we have referenced professional guidelines that may apply to you, but each clinician should investigate and understand the requirements governing his/her profession. In addition, be aware that laws and regulations may be federal, state, or municipal and will vary depending on where you conduct your business. Any resources listed in this book are for information only, and inclusion of such resources does not constitute endorsement by the author or publisher. Consult an attorney on matters specific to your business and situation.

Foreword

by Julie A. Jacobs, Psy.D., J.D.

One thing is certain – someday, you will stop providing mental health services to clients. Ideally, this will be an intentional choice to retire or to otherwise alter the course of your career. But for many people, there is no planning period for ceasing practice. Instead, something happens – an accident, illness, injury, or even death – that forces the sudden closing of a mental health practice.

As an attorney and psychologist who specializes in ethics and risk management consultations, I consult with mental health providers every day about a wide variety of issues related to their practices. However, few of my clinician clients bring up the question of how to plan for their unexpected death or incapacity. Despite the fact that many states, including my home state of Colorado, require mental health providers to have a plan in place for the disposition of their records and their practice in the event of their death or incapacity, few providers consider this as part of their overall practice planning. The providers I consult with have myriad questions about how to best care for their clients – issues of records releases, terminating or transferring care, advocating for their client's well-being – they clearly care deeply about their clients.

However, they usually fail to consider or plan for the impact of their absence on their clients.

When assisting a mental health provider with their informed consent paperwork, I always advise them to identify a "professional designee" who will manage their clients and records in the event of the provider's death. Most clinicians do not already have such a designee in place, and this is often the first time they have ever considered what they would do in this situation. However, once we begin that conversation, they quickly understand that this type of planning is part of their legal and ethical obligations to their clients.

The other way that I have seen clinicians become aware of this obligation is when a colleague unexpectedly dies or becomes incapacitated. In those situations, I often get a flurry of calls from the clinicians' colleagues – distressed, grieving, and unclear on how to best help. They know *something* should be done but is it often not clear exactly *what* needs to be done, and in the immediate aftermath of such an event it can be incredibly difficult to make appropriate and ethical decisions about next steps.

An essential way to relieve the burden and impact of this kind of event on your clients, colleagues, and families is to be proactive in developing a plan for the disposition of your records and of your practice in the event of your death or incapacity. While having a verbal agreement with a colleague to act in this role is a vital first step, it is not enough.

Reducing this plan to writing and formally appointing professional executors can have a number of benefits – it forces you to think in a systematic way about what needs to be done and how; it allows you to share important information with your professional executor(s) and avoids a frantic search for files, contact information, and the like; it relieves your family of the burden of navigating issues related to your practice at a time of stress and grief; it allows you to determine what information is shared with your clients and how that information is provided; and it gives you the peace of mind of knowing that you are not only meeting your ethical obligation to your clients, but you are also ensuring that a capable colleague will help them deal with your unexpected absence and an interruption in their care.

That is where this book comes into play. Cathy Wilson has put together an indispensable guide for mental health clinicians on how to think about and draft a professional will. Cathy reached out to me after the untimely death of a colleague reminded her of the importance of having a professional will in place. Instead of simply drafting a professional will for herself and considering the issue settled, Cathy recognized that her own challenging experiences in trying to deal with the aftermath of a colleague's death could have been made easier by the existence of a professional will. She became invested in helping her colleagues avoid being placed in the difficult position that she had found herself in, first by creating a workshop where clinicians in Colorado could draft their own professional wills, and now by authoring this wonderful resource for providers around the country and across the globe.

One Last Act: A Mental Health Clinician's Guide to Professional Wills is a straightforward and thorough resource for mental health providers who want to ensure that their clients, colleagues, and loved ones don't have to carry additional burdens in the event of their death or incapacity. Following Cathy's guidance will allow you to explore your own resistance to drafting a professional will; identify the person or people best equipped to act as your professional executor(s); think carefully and proactively about how you would want your clients to be notified and what information you would want shared with them; consider what other people and organizations need to be notified of the cessation of your practice; and provide the critical information your executor(s) will need in order to carry out your wishes.

After reading this book and engaging in a thorough analysis of your practice and the needs of your clients, you will be well-equipped to draft a professional will that will not only help address your legal and ethical obligations, but will also help you sleep better at night knowing you have taken care of this essential (and often avoided) task. I am very grateful to have this resource available to share with the providers with whom I work, and I know you will appreciate the guidance and insights contained here as well.

You've dedicated your career to taking care of others – you are a helper and a healer, a source of support and information. Now, with this one last act, you can continue to feel confident that you are doing your best to take care of your clients, colleagues, and family.

Julie A. Jacobs, Psy.D., J.D.
Owner, Julie A. Jacobs, PC
Risk Management Consultant, The Trust
Lyons, Colorado 2020

Introduction

This book is for mental health professionals who work directly with clients. As a clinician in this role, you should have some method of taking care of those clients in case something were to happen to prevent you from being able to work.

We create professional wills for this purpose. Some mental health professions may refer to their will as a contingency plan. It provides a way to allow another clinician to maintain your records or transition clients to new treatment in the event of your untimely death or incapacitation.

Yuck, right?

Your professional will may only be used temporarily if you are incapacitated for a short time. It also may become one of the last acts you will have performed to care for your clients.

It isn't fun to contemplate your premature death or any other sudden event that may keep you from working. However, it is an ethical responsibility, and in some places, a legal requirement, for any mental health professional to have a plan in place for this. It is also the right thing to do. Let me describe some things that could happen if you don't.

- A client arrives for their 9:00 a.m. appointment with their therapist. The therapist doesn't have a receptionist and the client is used to sitting in a waiting area until the therapist comes to get them. Ten minutes go by and this is strange because the therapist is never late, so the client texts her. No response. After 30 minutes with no word from the therapist, feeling a little upset, the client leaves. She sees an obituary a week later and realizes that her therapist died two days before they were supposed to meet. She is shocked, and also grieving now, and feeling guilty for being so angry when the appointment was missed.

- A client has been working hard with his therapist and feels a strong connection with her. He has a lot of trust in her support and has learned a lot about managing his mental health, but the issues he faces are significant enough that he has applied for disability. His application is coming close to the final stages of being approved, and his therapist has been preparing copies of his records to forward to his attorney. Before this can happen, she is involved in an accident and dies. He can't find anyone to help him with his records, and after weeks of trying, while also grieving the loss of someone who has been so important to him, he must seek out another therapist to start over.

These are situations that can be prevented by preparing a professional will.

This book is appropriate for mental health clinicians with any of the professional designations we may carry. These are a few of the designations for mental health professionals who work directly with clients:

- Professional Counselor
- Marriage and Family Therapist
- Clinical Social Worker
- Master's Level Psychotherapist
- Psychologist
- Psychiatrist
- Psychiatric Nurse Practitioner
- Addiction Counselor

Although these titles will vary, the general concepts in this book are appropriate for clinicians in any state or country in the world, although the specific legal and ethical requirements for a given professional will vary. This book focuses on the aspects of creating a professional will that relate to our clinical and ethical responsibilities. It provides a framework for how to think about this in terms of your own practice and clients. It is not intended to meet any potential legal requirements, and you are strongly encouraged to consult with your own attorney for legal guidance on such requirements. Please note the disclaimer at the beginning of this book.

I have filled this book with things to consider as you choose a Professional Executor, make decisions, and include information in your professional will. There are many decisions and tasks that will not only take care of your ethical responsibility to your clients, to the best of your ability without being able to predict the future, but will also ease the process for everyone who must be involved if you are suddenly not able to continue your practice.

It is my intention that this book will be a guide for you in making these decisions and creating a complete and accurate professional will that will give you, your family, and your colleagues peace of mind. I hope that it prompts you to think of information that would be needed, that you may not have thought of before. Also, I hope it gives you tools to make the necessary decisions ahead of time and prevent chaos in the event that someone has to unexpectedly step in and care for your clients.

My Background

I am a mental health counselor in Littleton, Colorado. I've been in private practice full time for about ten years now. In 2018, I created a workshop for colleagues to teach them how to complete their professional wills. My experience in creating the template for that workshop, the discussions during workshops, and the circumstances that led me to do it have all come together to result in this book.

I'd had a full private practice for years before I realized that I needed a professional will. I don't recall hearing any discussion about professional wills or contingency planning when I was in graduate school. I also don't recall any discussion of this in clinical supervision. Fortunately for me, I have been in a consultation group for many years with some talented professionals and the subject came up there.

In January 2017, a dear friend and colleague passed away suddenly. He and I had collaborated on some of our work in the few years before that and had grown to know each other well enough that I had asked him to be a Professional Executor on my own professional will.

Like many of my colleagues, when we discussed my professional will he made the comment, "I really need to get that done." I've also heard from many clinicians that before speaking to me about professional wills they hadn't known anything about them.

In the end, my friend didn't end up taking the time to create a professional will. He cared deeply for every one of his clients and put a great deal of his energy into the work he did with them each day. You'll find as you read this book, that this is one of the reasons many of us procrastinate about getting our professional wills done. The day after he passed away, there were two of us that did our best to figure out how to help his family and clients. Parts of that story are woven throughout this book, even though I may not directly say so in every example. I learned a lot from that experience.

My professional will remained unchanged, with him as one of my Professional Executors, until September of 2018. That month, another close colleague passed away. And again, it was sudden and unexpected. This loss was enough to finally motivate me to update my professional will. As I processed my grief with colleagues who were also grieving, the subject of a professional will came up many times. I heard that same phrase again, "I really need to get that done."

Along with the motivation to update my own will, this created a desire to help others get theirs done as well. Particularly since I found it was a very difficult process! There wasn't a cohesive resource to learn what I needed to do or how to prepare, so I resolved to create one. By November of 2018, I had created the first version of my professional will template and had facilitated a couple of workshops. These have been an incredible experience. I have loved getting to know each person and helping them complete this task. The work of helping mental health professionals complete a professional will has evolved now into this book.

I hope this book makes this "one last act" a little bit easier for you.

A professional will template is included with this book. You'll find it as an Appendix near the end of this book, and it is also available for download online from the *One Last Act* website at www.onelastact.net. Please use the password found at the beginning of Appendix I.

Part I
Get Ready!

Chapter 1:
What is a Professional Will?

“ A professional will is a plan for what happens if we die suddenly or become incapacitated without warning. It helps those whom we designate to respond to our clients' needs and to the unfinished business of our practice. It spells out decisive details that can be hard or impossible to come by at a time of shock and mourning.”[1] (Pope and Vasquez)

This is a good quote that briefly describes what a professional will is. The quote is from *Ethics in Psychotherapy and Counseling: A Practical Guide*, by Kenneth Pope and Melba Vasquez. Some professions may use other terms such as "Disposition Plan," "Record Disposition Plan," or "Contingency Plan."

Let's take the idea a bit further and talk about what that means and what is important for you to know before you start creating your own.

A professional will designates a clinician to handle your responsibilities to your clients if something happens to you.

It is important to note that the person named as your Professional Executor must be a clinician. Why? That person is going to be not only handling confidential client files, but they will also be talking with potentially bereaved clients. That person will need to be able to respond appropriately to clients' grief and they will need to be able to make appropriate referrals for continued care.

That person may also need to coordinate care if a client has multiple providers. They may need to provide copies of files or treatment summaries. All these tasks require a clinician who is aware of their ethical responsibilities and appropriate methods of client care.

A professional will is not the same as a personal will.

These two documents are very different. Your personal will is a document with instructions for how to handle your personal affairs and assets and may include designating a guardian for your children or other instructions according to your wishes.

Your professional will provides instructions, information, and your wishes only as they pertain to your clients and your practice.

Many people store these documents together, but their purposes remain distinct.

There are many resources available to complete a personal will and other concerns related to your personal life. The best resource would be an estate attorney. Other options you may be interested in exploring are:

- The "Five Wishes" living will template
- Living Wills
- Medical Powers of Attorney
- Advanced Directives

A professional will takes effect if you die, or if you are incapacitated.

Most of us understand that a professional will would come into effect if we die. It isn't as commonly known that it also can take effect if you are incapacitated. For instance, if you are in an accident and unable to contact your clients, a professional will authorizes your Professional

Executor to get access to your records and to contact clients. Clients may be coming in for appointments soon or contacting you for other reasons that would require a response.

A professional will provides instructions for how to handle your records, notification of clients, and other logistical and clinical issues.

Providing instructions to your Professional Executor can be invaluable. We all have a general idea of what is done in our work. We keep certain types of documents in client records, we handle clinical issues a certain way, and we have a calendar, so we know who we are seeing today. The instructions give your Professional Executor the specifics, though, of how *you* do business. How do you keep your calendar? Is it a paper calendar in a planner, or do you keep it on your smart phone's calendar app? Those are the most common methods, but you might like to use something entirely different.

That example is a relatively minor detail, but so important. The instructions you provide will help everyone with the minor and the major details of your practice.

Chapter 2:
What's the Big Deal?
What if I Don't Have One?

The short answer to this is that it is our ethical, and sometimes legal, responsibility to have a professional will in place. The ethical considerations include matters of continuity of care, avoiding harm to clients and others, confidentiality and privacy, and similar matters. Here are a few factors that demonstrate the importance of a professional will:

Chaos.

When a person is suddenly incapacitated or unexpectedly dies, the people in their life, including family, clients, colleagues and other acquaintances, often have a hard time dealing with the situation. Not having a professional will adds to the chaos. The opposite is true as well- when you do have one it can be a guide to follow in a time of uncertainty.

In my own experience, it would have eased a lot of chaos for us if we had known where to find my friend's calendar, where his keys were for his file cabinets, and if we had been able to intercept client calls instead of his family getting those calls. I know for certain that the family didn't mind, but I also know for certain that it was difficult to handle in the midst of their own grief.

Your family needs this.

In general, the people in our life that are not in mental health professions do not know about the things that need to be done for our clients. They may start calling clients themselves, answering client calls, or trying to gain access to client files in an effort to be helpful.

They could be overwhelmed when a client's grief-stricken response adds to their own grief and may also feel uncertain about what to do for a client. This adds to a family member's distress, and of course, we don't want that if we can help it.

It will already be difficult for clients.

An unexpected loss like this would be difficult enough for a client. We don't want to add to any client's distress by not being prepared.

There could be questions and confusion related to ethics and confidentiality if you don't have a professional will.

Without a professional will to designate a particular clinician to handle client records and to know client names and contact information, there can be questions, confusion, and concern about how to handle this situation, especially about confidentiality. Clinicians who aren't sure what to do, or receive incorrect or conflicting information might delay in accessing records or in notifying clients.

In the type of situations we are talking about, it may be that the clients' needs to be notified and their records maintained would outweigh the ethical need to be sure that we honor and protect the clients' confidentiality. But hey, many ethical dilemmas are a conflict between two ethical considerations! This perceived ethical dilemma is preventable by having a professional will in place.

HIPAA (Health Information Portability and Accountability Act) Compliance.

It isn't a direct HIPAA rule that every practitioner should have a professional will. What HIPAA does require (if your practice falls under HIPAA directives) is that each of us identifies and mitigates risks associated with keeping our client's records and protected health information (PHI) secure. Your death or incapacitation is a risk, and a professional will is one way to mitigate that risk. In the United States, providers who are Covered Entities must comply with HIPAA requirements. For those of you outside of the United States, this may not be a mandate but perhaps a "best practice."

For convenience, the Reference section of this book contains links to several of the United States ethical guidelines for different professions (Psychologists, Social Workers, Counselors, etc.).

Chapter 3:
What Holds Us Back from Getting This Done?

I have asked several colleagues about this question. For the most part, I only needed to look at my own behavior and thought processes to come up with the answer, but my colleagues confirmed what I already knew. Here are a few common reasons:

Procrastination.

This is definitely the most common reason I have heard, although it's been described in different ways. The way I see it, we procrastinate because of some or all of the reasons below.

Low priority compared to other responsibilities.

I want to emphasize this one pretty strongly. We have a lot of responsibilities and many of them are invisible to clients and other people we know. I've had people mention to me that I have an easy job because I "just talk to people all day." If only they really knew the investment we have in this work! There is so much background work that goes into what we do. That background work tends to be pretty invisible to others. For instance, we have documentation, billing, calling potential clients and managing client concerns outside of sessions, as well as coordinating care with other professionals.

If we are in private practice, there is another area of responsibility to keep up with – that of building our business and maintaining it. This could mean managing advertising, administrative tasks and more. It also entails tracking and managing billing and other administrative tasks associated with working with insurance companies. The more complex your business, the more background tasks that demand your attention.

The tasks and to-do's we have don't account for the emotional toll our work takes on us. Each of us must take care of ourselves, along with managing the business and client concerns. It is no surprise that tasks that don't have an immediate need, such as making a professional will, fall lower and lower on our priority lists.

It seems like a lot of work.

It can be a lot of work! At the same time, if you only have time to designate one Professional Executor and give that person some basic instructions, then just do that much. In this book, I have information that would allow you to make your professional will much more extensive than that, but that is one basic way to meet your ethical responsibility.

The complexity of your situation may be contributing to your procrastination as well. For instance, the task can seem more daunting the larger your practice, the more diverse your client population, and if you have a business partner or multiple people involved with your practice.

No matter how complex it seems or how complex it actually is, break down the tasks into smaller and more manageable work. Part Two of this book is all about decisions to make and preparing the will itself. Take it one section at a time, because it is essentially a step-by-step plan to get this done.

Issues or fears related to death or our own mortality.

We are in mental health, and we get it that this is a possibility. However, I've found that this is a pretty tough problem to overcome. If you think this might be happening for you, there is a reason, and working with your own therapist to uncover it will help you move through the block, and ultimately accomplish this task.

I think it is worth mentioning that for myself and a few of my colleagues, this was an unexpected roadblock to getting a professional will done. Until it came up in conversation, I didn't realize how much this was affecting me.

It is also easy to think this isn't very important...*yet.* If you are healthy and have a low-risk lifestyle, it just may not have occurred to you before picking up this book that you need to be prepared. However, there is a lot in our world that we can't control.

You have the training, plus you probably have a therapist of your own. Explore this, just in case it is one factor holding you back as well.

Not knowing you need one, or not knowing how to create one.

I've come across many colleagues who aren't aware that they need a professional will. I've also encountered many who didn't know how to create one. I didn't realize it myself until a few years after I started my private practice. It was in the ethics guidelines for my profession, but I missed it until it came up in a consultation group I have been part of for many years.

Fear of being judged if you allow a Professional Executor to see your files and how you operate.

Many of us worry about how we are perceived as a therapist and whether we are doing a good enough job in our career. You might think of this fear of being judged as a form of "imposter syndrome." It often appears that our colleagues are handling clients and business affairs better than we are.

If this is coming up for you, please remember that none of us are perfect. We all have strengths and weaknesses. Do your best to catch up, organize, and handle these types of details in your business. Your colleagues and others who matter to you will know you've done your best.

Difficulty choosing a colleague you trust to be a Professional Executor.

If you are reading this book, you take your responsibilities to your clients very seriously and want to do what is right by them. You know that asking someone to be your Professional Executor is asking that person to take on an important responsibility, and you want your clients taken care of gently and thoroughly.

If you are struggling with this, I would suggest joining a consultation group, becoming part of networking groups on social media or in person, and planning one-on-one meetings with colleagues to get to know some of them better. You will find someone!

Reluctance to impose on a colleague by asking them to be a Professional Executor.

While this concern may be somewhat of a surprise to you, I have found that it is pretty common to feel like it is an imposition to ask a colleague to be a Professional Executor. Some colleagues were not able to progress in getting their professional will done because of this.

This last roadblock is addressed in the next chapter.

Chapter 4:

Why Would A Colleague Want to be a Professional Executor?

T his has been a major concern for many colleagues because it can feel like an imposition to ask a colleague to be a Professional Executor. However, there are many reasons a person may want to provide this service for you. Here are a few:

- They care about you and want to help
- The two of you have agreed to be each other's Professional Executors
- They are providing this service to others for a fee
- They are able to take on new clients or have a strong network to help with referrals
- You both may serve a specific demographic and it is important to coordinate support

Let's go into some detail about the items on this list.

They care about you and want to help.

The most common reason a colleague may want to help you that I have heard of is that they care about you. You might be concerned that this will be a huge burden on your colleague, but consider the burden imposed on your colleagues if you don't have a professional will in place. The better prepared you are and the more complete your professional will is, the easier this task will be for your Professional Executor. Some other things you may want to consider that could make it easier on this person are:

- Have a fire drill-type of exercise with them at your office. This allows your Professional Executor to run through different aspects of taking care of your affairs if something has happened to you. Doing this together will enable you to see if any additions or corrections need to be made.
- Take photos of parts of your office such as your file cabinets, your keys or other parts of your clinical and professional world. Make notes associated with each of these to describe what your Professional Executor may need to do.
- Keep in touch with your Professional Executor on a regular basis. There may be aspects of your practice or clients that it would be good to alert that person to. Also, being aware of changes in the clinical aspect of your business would make it easier for that person to be able to step in and assist your clients in the most appropriate way.
- Plan to meet once a year to review the professional will and discuss concerns or changes.
- If there is a need to and a way to, identify "at-risk" clients so your Professional Executor can take this into account when addressing client needs.
- Have a system in place to update your will and any supporting documentation.

The two of you have agreed to be each other's Professional Executors.
This is also a very common reason people agree to do this work. It is mutually beneficial.

They are providing this service to others for a fee.

Although this hasn't happened with any colleagues I am associated with, the idea of offering "Professional Executor" or "Records Management" services as a paid service that is planned ahead of time is a possibility.

They are able to take on new clients or have a strong network to help with referrals.

In some situations, it is often appropriate that your clients become your Professional Executor's clients if something happens to you. For instance, when you have a high percentage of Spanish-speaking clients in a predominantly English-speaking area of the world, and you have specifically chosen your Professional Executor because they speak Spanish, it may feel very natural for those clients to start seeing your Professional Executor as their own counselor.

You both serve a specific demographic and it is important to coordinate support.

A good example of this is if you both speak a language that isn't commonly spoken in your area, just like in the example above. Another example may be that you specialize in a relatively uncommon disorder. In some areas of mental health, it is more difficult than usual to find a provider that has the skills and attributes a client needs. If your clients would have a particularly difficult time finding a new provider if something happens to you, choose your Professional Executor accordingly. It needs to be someone who understands these client needs and can help your clients navigate finding a new provider.

It may also help you ask a colleague for this if you can assure that person that you have a professional will prepared with detailed instructions. You can let the person know that you have made it as easy as possible. Sometimes a brief list, such as the one below that describes what will be expected, can help. Every situation is unique so your list may include additional information. These tasks are most common:

- Notify clients
- Provide referrals
- Copy or review records for clients if requested
- Notify licensing board, professional liability insurance, and other entities
- Retain records for the required time period

You can let your colleague know about certain things you have done to make this as easy as possible, such as maintaining a referral list or keeping your files organized and up to date.

Your colleague may be worried about being overwhelmed with taking care of these things unexpectedly. You can let your Professional Executor know that it is all right to ask for help from others, as long as it is another clinician that performs those acts.

You may consider preparing a letter as a formal request to someone to be a Professional Executor. This gives you an opportunity to respectfully ask and provide the details in writing. This may allow your colleague to review it and take time to consider your request, and make it easier for that person to agree to help you.

Chapter 5:
Options for Completing a
Professional Will

Y ou have several options for completing a professional will.

- Find a blank, basic one to download or copy, fill it out, and follow state or government requirements to make it legal
- Download one from your Electronic Health Record (EHR) provider
- Download one from a professional association or your professional liability insurance company
- Work with an attorney to create one
- Borrow one that a colleague has used and customize it for yourself
- Complete a workshop on this topic or work with a consultant
- Use this book and the template that comes with it

Whichever option you choose, your main concern should be that it serves your clients' needs if you are no longer able to work. Secondary to that, it should meet your professional requirements, plus any other requirements you may need to meet in the area you practice (state or local government, for instance).

You may also use the information in this book in combination with one of the other options to create a professional will that fits your needs. As you progress to the next section of this book where you will get your professional will completed, you also need to consider the complexity of your business or practice; consultation with an attorney may be important to ensure that you attend to all of the relevant considerations.

For most of us, even large group practices, working with the template included with this book is sufficient. It is comprehensive and has been more than adequate for most of my colleagues here in Colorado.

Part II
Get it Done!

Chapter 6:
Things to Think About First

B efore you write or complete your professional will, there are some things to consider and decisions to make. In this chapter, I've listed these decision areas and considerations, along with some ideas to help you decide. When you think through these things ahead of time, completing the professional will becomes much easier! Some of these issues have been mentioned before, but now we are in the working section of this book. I've provided space to allow you to write notes for yourself about each of these areas if you choose to do that, or you could keep notes in a notebook for when you prepare your professional will.

What happens to your practice/business if you die?

The most common thing that colleagues do is plan to have their practice or business dissolve upon their death. If this is the case, your Personal Representative, who is the person designated in your personal will to handle your affairs, is likely to be the one to complete the dissolution itself. This will generally not take place until all considerations have been taken care of for clients, records, billing, banking, and other business matters.

If you have a business partner or partners, you have probably already decided whether your share of the business will go to someone else or will be distributed among the partners.

You may have decided that your Professional Executor or another colleague can simply take over the business/practice, and whether they will or will not compensate your family in some way for this. (This might cause you to need to get an attorney's help to value your business).

There are many options here, and considering what will happen to your practice after your death can inform other decisions regarding the creation of your professional will. It can also help determine how much information you need to provide in your professional will.

_____

_____

_____

How complex is your practice? Do you have several business names?

The professional will template included with this book is comprehensive, and can be used with many different business situations including group practices, individual private practices, partnerships, and others. Typically, a person's name and all business names are listed on their professional will.

Remember that your professional will is intended to provide care for your clients and make it as easy as possible for your Professional Executor to implement that care. If very different things need to happen for clients in one practice/business versus another you own, you may need to consider having multiple professional wills, and/or consulting an attorney.

_____

_____

_____

Do you have a group practice? Does the practice or do the clinicians own client records?

Some group practices are set up so that the practice is the formal custodian of the records, and some are set up in a way that individual clinicians are the custodians of their own records. This is an important distinction to make in your professional will, as well as take this into consideration when you decide how much to compensate your Professional Executor. Employment laws in the location of your practice may affect this.

There may be additional details you need to add for your Professional Executor if you have a group practice.

_____

_____

_____

Is your client population unique or high-risk in some way? Are there certain considerations to make based on client issues you work with, such as "at-risk" clients, cultural concerns, languages spoken, or another concern?

You may need to choose one or more Professional Executors based on your client population and their needs. Some examples of "at-risk" client populations may be suicidal or terminally ill clients. You may consider it best to have a Professional Executor who is experienced with your population. You may think it best to have someone who understands how to deliver the message that you have suddenly passed away, and who is potentially even ready to take on these clients as their own.

Another common concern is when you have clients who speak a language that is not the primary language in your area. For instance, in Colorado, many therapists do not speak any language other than English. Colorado clinicians who have clients who only speak Spanish should take care to designate at least one of their Professional Executors who speaks Spanish as well, to best care for these clients.

If you work with clients who must obtain services involuntarily, this may be of concern as well in how you create your professional will.

List any client population concerns you have here, so these can be addressed in the appropriate section of your professional will.

_____

_____

_____

Have you designated at least one Professional Executor?

This person must be a clinician who has been trained in mental health and knows the ethical requirements you follow for record retention and other clinical considerations.

There are likely other factors you are considering for your Professional Executor. You need to trust that this person is competent, has enough experience in this work to be able to explain the situation to clients gently and appropriately, and a person who can address all relevant issues on your behalf.

Have you spoken with that person to make sure they are willing and able to do this if something happens to you?

_____

_____

_____

Do you want to designate just one, or two Professional Executors?

You can designate two Professional Executors, one as a primary and one as a secondary.

Clinicians often find it helpful to list two Professional Executors. For instance, if you are an owner or part owner for more than one business you may designate one Professional Executor for each of them.

It is also possible that you may designate a primary Professional Executor, but for some reason they are unable to perform these duties at the time. Having a secondary Professional Executor will help everyone involved to care for your clients.

Also, depending on the needs of your clients and your business, you can designate additional Professional Executors.

_____

_____

_____

Do you want to allow your Professional Executors to decide at the time whether they will work together (i.e. divide the work needed to care for your clients)?

If you have one practice, but a lot of clients, allowing your Professional Executors to divide the work necessary to care for your clients may make a lot of sense for you. In the professional will template included with this book, you can let them decide themselves at the time what is an appropriate way to manage the work.

Before deciding on this, as well as who your Professional Executors will be, it would be helpful to consider the personalities of these individuals and whether you feel they will work well together or not. If not, consider designating other Professional Executors, or designating the specific responsibilities each will have.

_____

_____

_____

What will you pay your Professional Executor(s)?

In the workshops I have facilitated, this has been a difficult decision for many clinicians. The main difficulty is not knowing how much work may be involved in the event of their death or incapacitation.

In general, for an individual operating their own private practice, many clinicians have been designating a flat fee to each Professional Executor for compensation to perform this service, to be paid out of their estate. The template with this book allows you to designate an hourly or flat fee and allows for the Professional Executor to bill the estate for any expenses incurred as a part of performing this service.

If you have a large practice, a higher than average number of clients, only one Professional Executor, or other considerations related to how much work may be involved, you may designate more or less in the amount you pay your Professional Executor. In essence, consider how much you are asking your Professional Executor to do, to decide how much compensation to provide.

To give you an idea of the time involved in my situation, my colleague and I spent approximately 110 hours of our time in the first few months after our colleague passed away. This time was in coordinating with his family, calling clients to notify and refer them, gathering referrals, conducting support groups, obtaining and reviewing his files, copying records for clients, contacting appropriate organizations to notify them (insurance companies, the state Board, etc.), and more. In addition, I do an annual review of his records to shred those that have reached the end of the retention period. I still have another ten years of doing this annual task.

There isn't any kind of "going rate" for this kind of service! You'll need to decide what feels right for you, and possibly discuss it with your Professional Executor(s) as well.

_____

_____

_____

Where will you need to keep copies of your Professional Will?

You will need to have multiple copies of your professional will available. At a minimum, your Personal Representative and your Professional Executor(s) will each need to have a copy. Keeping track of the number of copies you have and who possesses them will help you when you need to update the document for any reason.

Some examples of others you may want to have a copy (or other locations) are a safe deposit box, a safe in your home, or your attorney. There is a list of possibilities in the professional will template.

_____

_____

_____

Will your Professional Executor need additional documents such as a Power of Attorney or a Business Associate Agreement?

Depending on what you intend to happen to your business, your Executor or others may need additional documents. For instance, if your Executor is taking over your business and you are taking care of the legal requirements to make that happen, you may want to provide them with a Power of Attorney. It can be limited to business-related activities.

A very common document needed is a Business Associate Agreement. If you are in the United States and your clinical practice is a Covered Entity and must remain compliant with HIPAA practices, you and your Professional Executor(s) will need to sign a Business Associate Agreement. This protects you, your Executor, and your practice.

A link to information about Business Associate Agreements, which is available on the United States Health and Human Services website, is in the Resources section of this book and is available on the *One Last Act* website as well, www.onelastact.net.

The Business Associate Agreement is an agreement between two individuals who will both have access to clients' Protected Health Information (PHI) and indicates that both agree to follow appropriate HIPAA practices to protect that information.

_____

_____

_____

What is the best way (or ways) to provide notification for your clients?

There are multiple ways that clients may be notified in the event of your death or incapacitation. Obviously, a couple of things would ideally be done as quickly as possible, such as putting a notice on your office door and calling clients who are expecting to be seen that day or very soon.

The notice we placed on the door of my colleague was simple and gave no details, it indicated that he was unavailable and to please call as soon as possible for information, and gave one of our names and a contact number.

Some other things you may prefer or need based on your business could be changing the greeting on your voice mail or placing a notice on your website. This also depends on the disposition of your practice. If your practice/business isn't going to be dissolved, you wouldn't put any notice on voice mail or the website for the business, but you might for an individual voice mailbox for your clients.

How far back should your Professional Executor go in your caseload to contact clients?

This is another question that depends on your client population and how you approach this work as a clinician. For instance, for many of us, we have some clients that come in very infrequently or that return periodically to work through problems that naturally arise in life. For instance, I have a few clients who I see every couple of months. A clinician who works like this may ask that the Professional Executor go back three months in your calendar to notify any clients you have seen in that time frame. A shorter or longer time frame might make more sense for you.

There may also be requirements based on your professional designation or your local government that require other forms of notification.

You may also consider your client population or even specific clients in this as well. If you typically develop very deep connections with your clients, this could lengthen the time you want your Professional Executor to go back in your caseload. You may also have specific clients that, depending on their circumstances, might be on a list to be notified no matter how long it has been since you saw them.

You will want to consider this to decide what makes the most sense. A very common timeframe is going back three months to notify clients.

Note that what you prefer on this also could affect how much you plan to compensate your Professional Executor(s).

_____

_____

_____

Do you want to leave some form of message for your clients?

This is another tough area for many clinicians. You certainly don't have to leave any message at all, and as always, depending on your client population it may not be appropriate. However, many of us have written a short "wishing you the best, thank you for the honor of trusting me to guide you through this time in your life" kind of message to our clients.

If you work with kids or teens, it may feel very important to you to have a message in place to give them, to help them with processing the grief and the transition, and to gain closure as they move towards working with another therapist.

_____

_____

_____

Do you want clients to be invited to a memorial service for you?

I have found that many clinicians feel strongly one way or the other on this issue. It seems that this depends heavily on your theoretical orientation and approach in this work. Whether you are leaning towards this or not, let me add a few thoughts here for you to consider

- How would your family feel about your clients attending a service or memorial for you? Would it be a burden or a blessing?
- How will your clients typically handle it if they attend? If your clients deal with mental health issues that make it very difficult for them to regulate themselves, it may be too much for your family.
- You may consider asking your Professional Executor(s) to coordinate a separate support group or memorial get-together for your clients. This way, mental health

professionals can facilitate and be there to help clients handle strong emotions that may arise. It isn't easy to lose your therapist in this way! If it doesn't seem appropriate to have clients at the services your family has, and if your Professional Executor(s) are able to provide this, it allows your clients to have this as part of their grieving process. If you do ask for this, consider changing the compensation you offer to your Professional Executor(s).

_____

_____

_____

Chapter 7:

A Professional Will – Section by Section

In the following pages, the professional will template is reviewed section by section. Where appropriate, we refer to Chapter 6, and the ideas there that you will have already thought about. Otherwise, we describe the type of information you will add to your professional will in each area, if it applies to your situation, of course.

A few things to note about the structure of this template:

- You are not likely to need to use all the pages or sections in this template – you can leave entire pages blank if you need to and allow it to fit your unique needs.

- The first four pages are essentially the executable part of the document and, at a bare minimum, you might choose to use just that section and leave the details up to your Professional Executor(s).

- The remainder of the template consists of instructions and additional information such as contact information, logins or passwords, which organizations you use for different services, where to find things, and more information such as this. There is a lot of value in providing this type of information for your Professional Executor(s).

It can allow them to more easily find what they need and care for your clients the best way possible.

- The pdf file that is available with this book contains fillable fields so you can type up the entire document and then print it. After that, you can add the appropriate signatures to make it legal, according to the requirements of your state or local government.

- The pdf file will periodically be updated and could be slightly different than the images included in the following pages with instructions.

- Don't use this section to fill out your professional will. The images included in this chapter are for illustration purposes, and the print is smaller than it normally would be. It will be easier to either use the pdf file included with this book, or the full professional will template included in the Appendix of this book when you actually fill yours out to complete it. Also, not all parts of the professional will template are included in this chapter, just enough to provide an adequate explanation.

- As you progress through these images as examples, you'll see that the fillable fields you will find in the pdf file show up as blue boxes.

The Professional Will Template

1. *Cover page*

The cover page allows someone to easily find the information contained within this professional will. There is a space at the beginning to include your name, and your private practice name(s). It includes section titles and page numbers.

Mental Health Clinician Professional Will for:

Figure 1 - Professional Will Cover Page

Note that at the top of page 2 there's another shorter name field. When you add an abbreviated version of your name and practice in this field, it will show up on most of the remaining pages of the professional will where needed; just not the signature page.

Professional Will for:

Figure 2 - Professional Will - Name Field at Top of Most Pages

2. Page 2 - Designating Your Professional Executor(s)

The spaces for designating a Primary and a Secondary Professional Executor also include space for you to include contact information.

This document is to be used in the event of my inability to continue my clinical private practice due to incapacitation or death. This is not a substitute for a Personal Will and Testament. It is intended to give authority and instructions to my Professional Executor regarding my mental health practice and clients.

The persons who are designated to contact my clients and conduct all activities that must be done by a licensed clinician in the interest of my practice and clients, in the event I am unable to practice, are:

Primary Professional Executor:

Contact Information:

Secondary Professional Executor:

Contact Information:

Figure 3 - Professional Executor Designation

3. Page 2 - Professional Executors Can/Cannot Choose to Work Together, and Duties to Perform

There are buttons to select "yes" or "no" to allow your Professional Executors to work together or to let them know you prefer they do not do that.

In most cases, clinicians do allow this. If you have multiple businesses, however, or another concern such as wanting one Executor to work with your English-speaking clients while wanting the secondary Executor to work with your Spanish-speaking clients, then you will choose "no." If you need to explain, there is room to add information on page 8 of the professional will.

Note that these names are included in my disclosure document. It is my wish that if these parties feel it is most appropriate to cooperate and act as joint Professional Executors, they should do so:

Yes ⦿   No ◯

Figure 4 - Professional Executors Working Together

The following image shows the options for what duties you need your Professional Executor(s) to perform. Most people choose all of these except "Other."

Note that this and several other "checkbox" lists that are similar will have an "Other" option. I've included this option to make it easier to list something here that is out of the ordinary.

I grant my Professional Executor full authority to: (select all that apply)

☐ Contact and assist current and past clients to handle transfer or closing of client matters.

☐ Carry out activities deemed necessary to properly administer this Professional Will.

☐ Determine, delegate and authorize other persons to act as deemed necessary to properly administer this Professional Will.

☐ Act as custodian for my client files, or designate a licensed clinician who is willing and able to keep them secure and maintain them for the statutorily required period, currently seven years.

☐ Work with my Personal Representative to coordinate activities to carry out this Professional Will.

☐ Other: _____

Figure 5 - Professional Executor Duties

4. Page 2 - Your Personal Representative and Attorney Contact Information

You will want to include contact information for either your Personal Representative or your attorney, or both. At the least, you need to add someone here that your Professional Executor(s) can contact in the event that they either know or suspect that something has happened to you. Your Personal Representative and/or attorney will need to know how to contact your Professional Executor(s) as well. This field is intended to help them get in touch with each other.

My Personal Representative and/or Attorney is:

Figure 6 - Personal Representative and/or Attorney

5. *Page 3 - Location of Copies of Professional Will*

You will want to include who (individuals and organizations) has a copy of your professional will. For one thing, this will help you get copies to the right places if you need to update your professional will. Secondly, if your Executor needs to contact any of the others on the list, they will know if there is already a copy with that person or organization.

There are multiple copies of this Professional Will. They are located as follows: (check all that apply)

☐ In the possession of a Primary Professional Executor.

☐ In the possession of a Secondary Professional Executor.

☐ With my Personal Will and Testament.

☐ With my professional liability company.

☐ With my attorney.

☐ In my safe deposit box.

☐ With my EHR provider.

☐ With a clinical supervisor or employment supervisor.

☐ Other:

Figure 7 - Location of Copies of Professional Will

One Last Act – Part II

6. *Page 3 - Additional Documents You May Need*

Information about the Business Associate Agreement for HIPAA compliance and Power of Attorney documents were included in Chapter 6.

Additional documents you may need include a HIPAA Business Associate Agreement or Durable Power of Attorney for Business Affairs between myself and all Professional Executors listed, and if so they will be with this Professional Will. Other documents you may need:

Figure 8 - Additional Documents to Include with Your Professional Will

7. *Page 3 - Disposition of Your Business/Practice*

Information about this section was included in Chapter 6.

My intention for the disposition of my practice: (will another person inherit business, is it to be dissolved, etc.,note that this there is space to add more details in the Instructions section.

Figure 9 - Disposition of Your Practice

8. *Page 3 - Compensation Rate for Professional Executor(s)*

Information about this was included in Chapter 6.

You may bill my estate for your time and any other expenses that you may incur in execution of these instructions. Unless otherwise ordered by the court, the hourly◯ flat◉ rate of $ _____ is acknowledged to be fair and reasonable

Figure 10 - Professional Executor Compensation

9. Page 4 - Signature(s)

At the very least, of course, you will need to sign your professional will. This template includes space for two witnesses and for the document to be validated by a notary public. Your state or local government may not require that your professional will is notarized, but this would add protection if you choose to include that.

Note that this has been written with clinicians based in the United States (US) in mind, but an alternate signature page could be substituted if necessary. For example, if this will not work for locations outside of the US, it is important to know what may be legally required for the location you practice in.

Signature Page for the Professional Will of:

I declare, under the laws of the State of _____, that the foregoing is true and correct. Executed at

(location):

Print Name:

Signature: _____   Date: _____

Witness 1:

Print Name:

Full Address:

Telephone, Email:

Signature: _____   Date: _____

Witness 2:

Print Name:

Full Address:

Telephone, Email:

Signature: _____   Date: _____

State of _____,
County of _____

On _____, these parties: _____
_____
appeared before me, a Notary Public for the above state and county, and are known to me or provided photo identification and
that such individuals executed the foregoing instrument, and being duly sworn, such individuals acknowledged that they
executed said instrument for the purpose therein contained of their free will and voluntary act.

_____
(Signature of Notary Public)

My commission expires: _____

Figure 11 - Signature Page

10. Page 5 - Preferred Methods for Contacting Clients

This was discussed in Chapter 6, and note that, depending on which items you check in this list for notification, you can also add information on page 8 that gives more detail on what you prefer your Professional Executor(s) do.

☐	Place a notice on the door of my office, indicating my unavailability and to contact appropriate person.
☐	Call current clients.
☐	Call past clients up to ____ months in the past.
☐	Alter my voice mail greeting to advise clients calling for me to contact you.
☐	Place a notice on my website.
☐	Add an auto-responder to my email to advise clients or others contacting me as appropriate.
☐	Add a notice to social media:
☐	Other:

Figure 12 - Methods to Contact Clients

11. Page 5 - Message to be Given to Clients

This was also discussed in Chapter 6. If this isn't enough space, you can always add a page to your professional will or include additional information on page 8.

Message I would like given to my clients if appropriate to the circumstances (future best wishes, appreciation for them, etc. More may be attached to this professional will):

Figure 13 - Message to Clients

12. Page 5 - Inviting Clients to Memorial or Other Services

This was also discussed in Chapter 6. If you have concerns or aren't sure, check the "Ask family, or see below" option and add information to the text field.

| I wish for clients to be invited to my memorial service: | Yes ⊙ | No ○ | Ask family, or see below: ○ |

Figure 14 - Inviting Clients to Memorial or Other Services

13. Page 6 - Colleagues and Others to Notify

The following image is part of the page that includes colleagues and others to notify. The intention is that in the first field, you would add colleagues who it would be most important to notify right away. These might be others at a group practice where you work, an office mate or another person who may need to know right away.

When you get to this section of the professional will, you may want to review several pages ahead to get an idea of what the different fields are, to organize how colleagues and other associates will be listed.

Instructions: Contacting Colleagues and Other Professionals

Colleagues to be notified as soon as possible (include contact information):

Additional colleagues or other professionals/persons to be notified (include contact information and association with that person):

In my building/office:

In a professional organization/consultation group:

Figure 15 - Notifying Colleagues

14. Page 7 - Retention of Records

This text is included in the professional will, followed up with fields to let your Professional Executor know how and where you maintain your records.

Note the question at the end of the paragraph below. If your Professional Executor were to need to copy a lot of records for you, it would be helpful for there to already be an established fee for this service, so they can collect it.

> **Instructions: Client Record Retention**
>
> Client Records: Only if requested by clients, please arrange for copies of referred clients' records to go to their new therapists. It is my strong preference that you not give clients their records directly, but instead offer to send them to their new therapists. If a client insists on receiving a copy of their record, and it is your professional opinion that receiving the record will not result in significant harm, I ask that you meet with the client and go over the record together so you can assist the client in interpreting and understanding the information in their record. All records must be maintained for the statutorily required period, currently seven years, after termination of the treatment or the last client visit. I do ● do not ○ have a fee associated with copying records in my disclosure.

Figure 16 - Client Records

15. Page 8 - Other Pertinent Information Professional Executors Need

On page 8 of the professional will template, there is a large field that can hold many lines of text. This can be a catch-all field to refer to in case any of the other fields are not quite enough to get all the information on this document that you need to. For most clinicians, this has been enough, and they have not needed to add additional pages to their professional will.

Instructions: Additional Information

Other information you may need is included below. This may pertain to the disposition of my practice, information about specific client populations I work with, or other information I feel is important for you to know:

Figure 17 - Additional Information Field on Page 8

16. Page 9 - Access to Office, Records, and Information

Part of page 9 is included in the image below, to give you an idea of the type of fields and information to provide here. Depending on what you intend to happen to your practice, you may choose to fill in some very specific information or choose to withhold some information (such as passwords). For example, if your practice will be dissolved, some tasks will need to be handled by your Personal Representative, and not your Professional Executor. Keep this in mind as you complete these sections.

Even if your Professional Executor(s) doesn't need the information, you might decide to list some items anyway for convenience.

Also, keep in mind that the more information you provide in this section and the following sections, the more secure you must keep this document. Be wary of emailing it and be careful where you store copies of it. Advise everyone who has a copy to be careful as well. In addition, if you do provide passwords, you will need to ensure that they are kept up-to-date in this document.

Access to Office, Records, and Information

The following information is gathered to help you find what you need to accomplish the immediate tasks such as notifying clients and locating records, keys, etc. (attach additional information if necessary

Voice mail access information and password:

Email access information and password:

Website access information and password: (only if need to update website for client)

Location of other passwords needed (for instance, do you have a "password manager" app):

Figure 18 - Access to Office, Records, and Information

17. Page 10 - Personal and Business Identifying Information

In this section, you'll add information that your Professional Executor(s) will need to identify you when referring to your accounts, your credentials with insurance companies and other arrangements they will need to make. It is noted in the professional will that many things need to be canceled, such as your license with your licensing board, your NPI, your professional liability insurance, or credentialing with insurance companies.

Note: At least some of this work may be legally more appropriate for a Personal Representative to handle. However, since a Professional Executor must be a clinician, the language and processes are more familiar to those in the profession than they might be to a family member. When I acted in a Professional Executor's role, I worked with DORA (Colorado's Department of Regulatory Agency that manages licenses in our state),

NPPES (National Plan and Provider Enumeration System, the organization that manages NPIs), and Medicaid and insurance companies to handle the deactivation of these items. It would have been confusing and frustrating for my friend's family members.

Many of these would likely be canceled eventually without your Professional Executor initiating that process. One critical item is your NPI(s), or National Provider Identifier. You may have a similar identifying number if you are not in the United States (US).

This is critical in order to prevent insurance fraud. All insurance claims in the US are processed with at least one NPI, either an individual or Type 1 NPI, or a group or Type 2 NPI. Your Professional Executor(s) will need to submit a form to deactivate each NPI you have, so list them all on your professional will. The link to submit a request to deactivate is included on the professional will.

Without deactivating this, someone with the right information could submit insurance claims under your NPI and potentially be paid. To be on the safe side, it would be a best practice to request that your Professional Executor(s) contacts each insurance company, and any other third-party payers you work with, to notify them.

If you are outside the US, investigating whether there is a similar system where you have your practice would be wise so that a similar identifying number or account could be canceled.

Note that you may or may not be canceling a group NPI, or contracts with insurance companies, depending on what you have decided will happen to your business.

Personal and Business Identifying Information

Individual name:

Business name (include legal and dba names, any/all information needed to find with Secretary of State):

Office address(es) (attach sheet with additional locations if needed):

Office telephone number(s):

Office email address(es):

Tax ID:

Figure 19 - Personal and Business Identifying Information

18.Pages 11-13 - Contacts for Organizations You Do Business With

This section is full of potential businesses or individuals you work with, either by providing a service to them (such as teletherapy/telehealth through BetterHelp), or them providing a service to you (such as professional liability insurance, merchant services or a clearinghouse). Depending on what will happen to your business, you may or may not need to cancel accounts or services.

Even if you don't choose to list logins or passwords for any reason, at least list the organizations that you work with. This can be invaluable for whoever has to take any form of action.

Figure 20 - Other Business Information

19. Pages 14-15 - Office Processes, Assets, and Liabilities

The information contained in this section is the least likely of all to be used. It is likely to only be needed if a Professional Executor is taking over your business, such as someone who is already a partner.

You may only complete sections that relate to personal assets, or information pertinent to canceling a lease. Think about what your Professional Executor(s) might not already know from other sources and include that. For instance, if you share the lease for an office with someone, noting here which personal possessions are yours and should be given to your family would be important.

As before, you may choose to list information here that could be helpful to anyone working on closing or continuing your business, even if there is no identifying information.

Please note that some or all of the following information may be left blank depending on the disposition of the practice or circumstances. *If your Professional Executor is joining or taking over the business, he or she will need this information. In most circumstances, all that is likely to be needed is to designate any details about your personal property that is in your office.*

Liabilities - Office Lease (location, term, contract, contacts):

Liabilities - Office Lease (as above, for a second location):

Liabilities - Additional Leases (furniture, equipment, etc.):

Liabilities - Other:

Assets - Subleases:

Figure 21 - Business Assets and Liabilities

Chapter 8:
Additional Tasks

I n addition to completing your professional will, there are a few extra tasks that you may also need to do. These are not a direct part of the professional will, so they are listed separately to help you manage them. There may be other tasks you need to complete that are not listed here, and in case you are using this book as your workbook, I have included space for you to add them. These may be state or local requirements or a requirement of an employer or other organization you work with.

1. *Add your Professional Executors to your disclosure and informed consent form.*

Whether it is required in any way or not, it is good practice to add your Professional Executor(s) to your disclosure and informed consent form you use with your clients. The reason I say this is because it is always possible that a client knows one of your Professional Executors and may not want that person to be able to access their records. Any particular client may want to opt to restrict one of your Professional

Executors from access, and if so, you can note it in their record. You may also want to note that on your professional will itself.

2. *Notify existing clients.*

Just as with #1 above, any particular client may want to restrict one of your Professional Executors from having access to their records. Once you complete your professional will, notify each active client of its going into effect so they have the chance to ask you to restrict one or the other of your Professional Executors from having access to their records.

It probably isn't practical for you to contact every single client you have had that you still have to maintain a record for, but if you know of a client that may know one of your Professional Executors, it is probably worthwhile to contact that person to check, if you still possess their records. For instance, this may be a client that one of your Professional Executors referred to you.

3. *Add a fee for copying records to your disclosure document.*

In Chapter 7, there is a notation that you need to indicate in your professional will that you do, or do not, have a fee in your disclosure document to copy records. If you didn't already have one, you may decide to add this to your disclosure to protect both yourself now, and possibly your Professional Executor in the future so you don't have to provide this service at no charge. Be aware that federal and state laws limit the amount you can charge for copying records, so be sure to research the relevant laws in your area in order to ensure that you do not exceed these limits.

4. *Add to an operation or business processes manual you use in your practice.*

If you maintain an operations manual or business processes manual of any kind for your practice (for instance, if you operate a group practice), you may want to add Professional Executors in this manual.

Alternatively, if you have employees, you may want to make it a practice to add their professional will to their personnel file and require a new one any time it is updated.

This also allows you to review these to be certain they are in accordance with how you operate your business.

5. Contact your attorney, professional liability company, or EHR provider.

It may be helpful and appropriate to notify certain people or organizations of who your Professional Executors are, whether you provide a copy to that person or organization or not.

6. Get a legal business valuation on your practice.

If you made decisions in this process that would require you and others to know the true value of your business, that is also an extra task that will need to be done. You may also set yourself a reminder to revalue the practice at a regular interval as well.

7. Get into a consultation group.

I have gained more by being part of a consultation group than I ever expected. I have mentioned a few times that I didn't realize I needed a professional will, or even what that was until it came up in a consultation group I am part of. There are many other unexpected moments of learning and clarity that come from consulting with colleagues. Find one. Join and participate. The most fulfilled and successful therapists I know have made consultation a priority in their practice.

In case you haven't asked anyone yet to be a primary or secondary Professional Executor, this is a great way to build connections with your colleagues and find someone willing to perform this valuable service for you.

8. Other tasks associated with state or local government requirements.

_____

_____

_____

9. *Other tasks associated with a certifying or professional organization.*

_____

_____

_____

10. *Other tasks associated with an employment or independent contractor organization you work with.*

_____

_____

_____

11. *Put a date on your calendar to review your professional will!*

At a minimum, put a date on your calendar to go back over your professional will and update items that may need it. If you have agreed to do any other forms of checking in with your Professional Executor(s), put the date for this on your calendar as well.

Part III

It's Done!

Chapter 9:
Maintaining

Now that you have your professional will done (Yes!), it is time to consider what plans you need to make, and things you need to manage, to maintain the information and your practice appropriately.

At the end of the last chapter, you set a date to review your professional will and make any updates that may be necessary. Here are a few other considerations to think about.

What agreements do you have with your Professional Executor(s)? These may be:

- An annual review
- A "fire drill" type exercise to run through what tasks they would need to do
- Checking in when significant changes occur such as moving your office or offering a new clinical intervention (changing your client population)
- Checking in when you hear of legal changes that could affect your practice
- Checking in to be certain both of you still want to maintain this agreement

Beyond these items, you'll want to keep on doing what you are doing. If one of your Professional Executors needs to step in for you, these things make it easiest for them:

- Maintaining your records
- Deleting/shredding files when the retention period is reached
- Keep your passwords up to date (consider using a password management app for this)
- If anything of concern comes up, just write it in on your professional will if you must! It doesn't have to look perfect, but it should just make things easier.
- Include this book with your professional will and other documents in case your Professional Executor(s) need to refer to it.

As a reminder from Chapter 4:

- Have a fire drill type of exercise with them at your office. This allows your Professional Executor to run through different aspects of taking care of your affairs if something has happened to you. Doing this together allows you to see if any additions or corrections need to be made.
- Take photos of parts of your office such as your file cabinets, your keys or other parts of your clinical and professional world. Make notes associated with each of these to describe what your Professional Executor may need to do. You may want to update these.
- Keep in touch with your Professional Executor on a regular basis. There may be aspects of your practice or clients that it would be good to alert that person to. Also, being aware of changes in the clinical aspect of your business goes a long way towards that person being able to step in and assist your clients most appropriately.
- Plan to meet once a year to review the professional will and discuss concerns or changes.
- If there is a need to and a way to, identify "at-risk" clients so that your Professional Executor can take this into account when addressing clients' needs.
- Have a system in place to update your will and any supporting documentation.

Chapter 10:
For Professional Executors

I f you are a Professional Executor and are suddenly in the position of caring for a colleague's clients, this chapter is for you.

First, I am sorry this has happened, because you are likely grieving if your friend and colleague has passed, or worried about your friend if they have been incapacitated in some way.

Second, I hope the following list provides you with some helpful information whether you have a professional will to guide you or not.

Please know this, I've been there, and it can become very chaotic and difficult. On top of that, you are most likely to be grieving yourself. Do your best with these items as time goes on and remember that self-care is important, too. It took months before I felt more like myself again even though I took care of much fewer responsibilities at the time of my friend's death than a colleague of mine did. It is now two years later, and I am still working on some tasks associated with my friend's practice. If you need help, ask for it! If I can be of help, please don't hesitate to contact me for consultation.

- **Security and Protected Health Information (PHI)**

  Take care to secure records you receive, and be careful of what you share. It can be chaotic during this time, and it is very easy to forget the need to be discreet at a memorial service or on a phone call you receive. It is also easy to forget that you may not have appropriate releases in place to share information. This applies to colleagues as well as individuals or possible clients of your friend that you meet.

- **Referring Clients**

  When my friend passed away, there were two of us helping the family to take care of clients and clinical concerns. We created a list of colleagues to refer clients to and handed a copy to each person that asked. We had a list of colleagues we trusted that took different insurances and were in different locations. It helped a lot to have a list prepared, and not have to try to remember which clinicians had taken which insurance. It was hard enough as it was, and not having to recall these details in the moment was helpful.

- **Supporting Clients**

  The family generously allowed clients to attend any of the services for my friend that they wished. My colleague and I made it a priority for at least one of us to be available at those services and be ready to assist if it seemed that any clients needed it. We also scheduled two free support and memorial service groups for clients to attend if they wished. We each stayed in contact with some clients who seemed to need additional support. You may consider doing something along these lines as well, if your schedule, your time, and your energy allow.

- **Review Record Retention Requirements**

  If you aren't already certain of them, review record retention requirements you will need to follow. As I have sorted through records to maintain, it has been helpful to have the requirements clear in my mind (particularly for minors since my friend had a lot of children and adolescents for clients).

- **Record Requests and Redacting Pens!**

  It is also important to know what you can and cannot release, even when a client gives you an appropriate release of information consent form. Review your state or local laws or guidelines on this, as it applies to any request you receive. Also, read through every document you plan to release to someone. There may be portions that should not be readable in documents you copy, and you are allowed to redact these portions. Did you know there is such a thing as a redacting pen? They provide a more complete "blacking out" of portions of a record and should be used if you can obtain one. If your colleague has allowed for a

fee to copy records in their disclosure, you can charge for the time you spend doing this.

- **Document Your Work in Client Records**

    You can add documentation to client records (at least in Colorado you can), and you should do this if you act in any way on behalf of that client. If you copy records for the client, add a clinical note to indicate this with the date and all pertinent information. You may also add a note for any other interaction with the client that you feel is significant.

- **Consider Converting to Digital Records**

    My friend had a LOT of records, all in paper form. Although by the time I got around to checking to see if there were any files I could purge due to the retention period being over, there was still quite a lot of paper. I am currently in the process of converting the remaining records to digital form, and what a relief it has been on the space I have in my office! I am converting them to secure digital files, with appropriate and HIPAA compliant protection and backups. If you are interested in converting paper records to digital format, be aware that some states have laws/regulations about whether or not you can destroy the paper files; in addition, Medicare and other private insurers may have guidance about this. Be sure to research the laws and contractual requirements about this issue before destroying paper records.

- **If Records Are with an EHR**

    Remember to download all client data into a format you can use before canceling the account! Once you cancel it, the records are gone.

- **Professional Liability Insurance**

    You may be able to arrange for continued coverage if your colleague hasn't arranged for it already. Call the company to ask about provisions for "tail coverage," which allows for an extended reporting time if needed. "Tail coverage" is a provision that allows for claims to be filed after the policy is cancelled or expired, for incidents that happened during the active coverage period.

- **NPI**

    Ideally, as a Professional Executor, you would follow up on every account and organization your colleague worked with. Realistically, this is unlikely! One high priority item, however, is to deactivate any NPIs your colleague was using. This includes both Type 1 or individual NPIs or Type 2 or organizational NPIs. As of this writing, the link to download the form needed to deactivate an NPI is here: www.cms.gov/Medicare/CMS-Forms/CMS-Forms/downloads/cms10114.pdf It is important to deactivate NPIs to prevent insurance fraud. Without them being deactivated, with the right information, someone could use that NPI to submit a fraudulent insurance claim and potentially get paid.

- ***If the Business is Being Dissolved***

  Ask the Personal Representative to wait to complete the process of dissolving the business until all billing has been taken care of and all business-related affairs have been resolved.

Chapter 11:
Conclusion

Whether you are creating a professional will or acting as a Professional Executor, my heart goes out to you. It isn't easy to contemplate your premature death and what may need to happen afterward. It also isn't easy to consider how difficult a time like that may be for your clients and colleagues, let alone your family. When acting as a Professional Executor, it also isn't easy to pick up the pieces when a friend and colleague suddenly dies or is incapacitated.

As you go through the process of writing your professional will or caring for clients on behalf of a friend, this is definitely a time to keep self-care in mind. Our work takes a toll on us, even in the usual circumstances, let alone when you are worried or grieving for a friend and colleague, and carrying a heavier workload.

One other factor I would like to address as I conclude writing this book is raising awareness about the need for having a professional will.

I don't recall discussing professional wills in any part of my graduate program or in clinical supervision while I was working towards my license. I can't speak for everyone, but I have heard this same sentiment from many colleagues. I realize that this is one small factor in being a clinician, but it can have a tremendous and negative impact when it isn't taken care of.

Thankfully for me, consulting with peers in various ways is a priority for me, and this is how I learned of the need to have my own professional will.

Perhaps this could be an area we can improve in our field. It could look like any of these or all of these:

- Counseling graduate programs could incorporate discussion of professional wills and why they are important in their ethics courses.
- Counseling graduate programs may even incorporate a course or track on building a private practice, and professional wills would be one aspect of what future clinicians learn.
- Clinical supervisors would incorporate discussion of professional wills and their importance, and this would be required to sign off on a clinician's hours towards licensure. One clinical supervisor I know requires this at the beginning of supervision and the supervisee is given a deadline. She offers to be Professional Executor for them during supervision, and then before she signs off on the hours for licensure, she requires that the supervisee provide proof of having a new Professional Executor and active professional will.
- Adding professional wills to clinical supervisor training, especially for training that prepares a person for supervision credentialing.
- If you conduct a consultation group, you may consider it best practices to bring up professional wills at some point, and possibly even collaborate to help everyone complete their own professional will or be Professional Executors for each other.
- Adding this requirement to state licensure requirements in the form of requiring that licensees attest to having one in place. For instance, in Oregon, you must designate a person who will retain your records for you in case something happens to you, as a part of the licensing process.
- Providing training in the form of continuing education.

It is part of our ethical guidelines, but it seems like we could encourage clinicians in more ways to create their professional will, to avoid what could happen if you don't take care of this important task.

I wish you all the very best in getting this "one last act" done and feeling some peace of mind. In the event you need it, your clients will be cared for, thanks to your thoughtfulness and the efforts of your trusted colleagues.

Appendix I: Professional Will Template

T he following pages contain each page from the professional will template included with this book. Follow the below link to complete an editable PDF version of the professional will template. Use the password "yougotthis" to access the template.:

www.lifepathscounseling.com/PWW/OneLastAct-ProfWillTemplate.pdf

You can also download it by going to the *One Last Act* website at www.onelastact.net. Please use the password "yougotthis" to access the template.

Mental Health Clinician Professional Will for:

Contents:

Initials _____

This document is to be used in the event of my inability to continue my clinical private practice due to incapacitation or death. This is not a substitute for a Personal Will and Testament. It is intended to give authority and instructions to my Professional Executor regarding my mental health practice and clients.

The persons who are designated to contact my clients and conduct all activities that must be done by a licensed clinician in the interest of my practice and clients, in the event I am unable to practice, are:

Primary Professional Executor:

Contact Information:

Secondary Professional Executor:

Contact Information:

Note that these names are included in my disclosure document. It is my wish that if these parties feel it is

most appropriate to cooperate and act as joint Professional Executors, they should do so:

Yes ◯   No ◯

I grant my Professional Executor full authority to: (select all that apply)

☐ Contact and assist current and past clients to handle transfer or closing of client matters.

☐ Carry out activities deemed necessary to properly administer this Professional Will.

☐ Determine, delegate and authorize other persons to act as deemed necessary to properly administer this Professional Will.

☐ Act as custodian for my client files, or designate a licensed clinician who is willing and able to keep them secure and maintain them for the statutorily required period, currently seven years.

☐ Work with my Personal Representative to coordinate activities to carry out this Professional Will.

☐ Other:

My Personal Representative and/or Attorney is:

Initials _____

Message and Instructions to my Professional Executor(s):

First of all, I deeply appreciate your willingness to serve as a Professional Executor for this Will.

There are multiple copies of this Professional Will. They are located as follows: (check all that apply)

- ☐ In the possession of a Primary Professional Executor.
- ☐ In the possession of a Secondary Professional Executor.
- ☐ With my Personal Will and Testament.
- ☐ With my professional liability company.
- ☐ With my attorney.
- ☐ In my safe deposit box.
- ☐ With my EHR provider.
- ☐ With a clinical supervisor or employment supervisor.
- ☐ Other:

Additional documents you may need include a HIPAA Business Associate Agreement or Durable Power of Attorney for Business Affairs between myself and all Professional Executors listed, and if so they will be with this Professional Will. Other documents you may need:

My intention for the disposition of my practice: (will another person inherit business, is it to be dissolved, etc.,note that this there is space to add more details in the Instructions section.

You may bill my estate for your time and any other expenses that you may incur in execution of these instructions. Unless otherwise ordered by the court, the hourly ◯ flat ● rate of $ _____ is acknowledged to be fair and reasonable

Initials _____

Signature Page for the Professional Will of:

I declare, under the laws of the State of _____, that the foregoing is true and correct. Executed at

(location):

Print Name:

Signature: _____   Date: _____

Witness 1:

Print Name:

Full Address:

Telephone, Email:

Signature: _____   Date: _____

Witness 2:

Print Name:

Full Address:

Telephone, Email:

Signature: _____   Date: _____

State of _____,
County of _____

On _____, these parties: _____

_____
appeared before me, a Notary Public for the above state and county, and are known to me or provided photo identification and that such individuals executed the foregoing instrument, and being duly sworn, such individuals acknowledged that they executed said instrument for the purpose therein contained of their free will and voluntary act.

_____
(Signature of Notary Public)

My commission expires: _____

Remember to initial every page!

Initials _____

Instructions: Contacting Clients

Please use your best judgment/discretion in deciding the most appropriate and compassionate way of notifying current and past clients, as well as others. I trust your judgment. My preferences are indicated below; if you feel it is necessary to make additional or different efforts, please do so (information on how to access my voice mail, other records, etc. is in the section titled: "Access to Office, Records, and Information").

You can delegate some of these tasks to others, as appropriate. For instance, you may ask an office mate of mine to place a notice on the door of my office for you; or you may ask someone else to change the greeting on voice mail or place a notice on my website. How you can notify my clients: (please provide as much detail as necessary, for both current and past clients):

- ☐ Place a notice on the door of my office, indicating my unavailability and to contact appropriate person.
- ☐ Call current clients.
- ☐ Call past clients up to _____ months in the past.
- ☐ Alter my voice mail greeting to advise clients calling for me to contact you.
- ☐ Place a notice on my website.
- ☐ Add an auto-responder to my email to advise clients or others contacting me as appropriate.
- ☐ Add a notice to social media:
- ☐ Other:

Where to find contact information for clients:

Please provide 2-3 clinician referrals as appropriate to the disposition of my practice, and appropriate to the client's needs. Of course, please include yourself as a referral if it is appropriate. Note that some clients may not be ready for a referral until a later date.

Please use your best judgment and discretion in deciding how much information to give clients about my death or incapacitation (i.e. some circumstances could be triggering for clients).

Message I would like given to my clients if appropriate to the circumstances (future best wishes, appreciation for them, etc. More may be attached to this professional will):

I wish for clients to be invited to my memorial service: Yes ⦿ No ◯ Ask family, or see below: ◯

Initials _____

Instructions: Contacting Colleagues and Other Professionals

Colleagues to be notified as soon as possible (include contact information):

Additional colleagues or other professionals/persons to be notified (include contact information and association with that person):

In my building/office:

In a professional organization/consultation group:

Collaborator, coach, clinical supervisor, my own therapist, close associate, someone I'm a Professional Executor for :

Supervisees:

Employees/employer/office manager:

Others:

Initials _____

Professional Will for:

Instructions: Client Record Retention

Client Records: Only if requested by clients, please arrange for copies of referred clients' records to go to their new therapists. It is my strong preference that you not give clients their records directly, but instead offer to send them to their new therapists. If a client insists on receiving a copy of their record, and it is your professional opinion that receiving the record will not result in significant harm, I ask that you meet with the client and go over the record together so you can assist the client in interpreting and understanding the information in their record. All records must be maintained for the statutorily required period, currently seven years, after termination of the treatment or the last client visit. I do (●) or not ( ) have a fee associated with copying records in my disclosure.

Additional information or instructions related to client records (note anyone you are a Professional Executor for as well as: whether you already have their records, or if the person is still operating their practice and needs to be notified; information regarding those records that your Professional Executor needs to know):

Location of schedule of current client appointments (include any necessary access codes or instructions):

Location of current client records:

Location of past/archived client records (note that the current statutory requirements is to maintain records for seven years after termination in a safe, locked, secure location):

Location of process notes if not part of clients records (if maintained separate from record, these are not to ever be released to anyone, for any reason):

Initials _____

Instructions: Additional Information

Other information you may need is included below. This may pertain to the disposition of my practice, information about specific client populations I work with, or other information I feel is important for you to know:

Note:

You may not need all of the information contained in this document, as the primary intent is to designate appropriate professionals to notify my clients, refer them appropriately, and maintain the records for those clients for the statutorily appropriate time; as well as to work with my Personal Representative to advise on mental health ethics and standards of practice. The information contained in this document may be useful reference for both you and my Personal Representative.

I have expressed my preferences here throughout this document, and tried to include information that I feel would be helpful to you in deciding how to handle different circumstances. Overall, please know that I trust your judgment.

Initials _____

Access to Office, Records, and Information

The following information is gathered to help you find what you need to accomplish the immediate tasks such as notifying clients and locating records, keys, etc. (attach additional information if necessary

Voice mail access information and password:

Email access information and password:

Website access information and password: (only if need to update website for client)

Location of other passwords needed (for instance, do you have a "password manager" app):

Location of or actual computer password:

Location of answers to security questions (mother's maiden name, etc.:

Location of office keys (building, suite/office, filing cabinet, storage facility, etc.:

Information needed to access office space (notify receptionist or attendant, key code access, out of hours access, etc.):

Location of business records: (leases, insurance, license, etc.)

Location and access to storage unit, facility, or room:

For assistance in locating or accessing any of these records, contact:

Documents you may need (operation manual, disclosure, contracts, etc.):

Initials _____

Personal and Business Identifying Information

Individual name:

Business name (include legal and dba names, any/all information needed to find with Secretary of State):

Office address(es) (attach sheet with additional locations if needed):

Office telephone number(s):

Office email address(es):

Tax ID:

SSN:

Licenses (please list all with state and ID number, include login/password if this exists):
(Professional Executor will need to notify each licensing body such as Colorado DORA, 303-894-7855, 1560 Broadway, Denver, CO 80202)

Certifications (please list all with ID number and contact information for organization-such as NBCC for NCC or Nationally Certified Counselor):
(Professional Executor will need to notify each certifying organization)

CAQH:

Individual NPI (NPI-1):

Group/Organizational NPI (NPI-2):

(Professional Executor will need to use the form at this link to deactivate NPI's - it is important to do this to prevent the numbers being used for insurance fraud)

https://www.cms.gov/Medicare/CMS-Forms/CMS-Forms/downloads/cms10114.pdf

Initials _____

Professional Contacts

Please note that some of the following information may be left blank depending on the disposition of the practice, circumstances, etc. Institution name, individual name, website, contact information and other notes, passwords needed is provided as appropriate.

Office Leasing Agent:

Office Leasing Agent (second location - attach sheet with additional locations):

Professional Liability Company:
(Professional Executor please notify this carrier in writing as expeditiously as possible and arrange for extended reporting period if possible to protect my estate from future malpractice suits, or make other appropriate arrangements)

Other Insurance (general liability, etc.)

Professional Accountant:

Accounting Software or Service Provider:

Professional Attorney:

Banking Institution (1):

Banking Institution (2):

Initials _____

Merchant Services:

Credit Card (1):

Credit Card (2):

Payroll Services:

Clearinghouse or Insurance Billing Provider:

Government Taxes (local, payroll, etc.):

EHR (Electronic Health Record) Provider (note-do not cancel this until all records are retrieved):

CRM (Customer Relationship Management) Provider:

Psychological Testing Service Provider (or other clinical support service provider):

Janitorial Service Provider:

Initials _____

Website Hosting and/or Website Management Provider (may be one or more individuals/organizations):

Internet Service Provider(s):

Telephone Provider(s):

Fax Service Provider(s):

Cloud Storage Provider(s):

Professional Organizations (include website or other contact information):

Advertising Accounts (include website or other contact information):

Social Media Accounts:

Teletherapy Accounts, Associations, Organizations (VSee, BetterHelp, Talkspace):

Insurance companies/EAP/Medicaid/third party payors I am paneled with:

Confidential Document
Created by Cathy Wilson, LifePaths PLLC © 2020
Initials _____

Business Processes, Assets, Liabilities

Please note that some of the following information may be left blank depending on the disposition of the practice or circumstances. ***Most likely this is only needed if the Professional Executor is taking over/joining the business.***

Structure of client records (do you keep your process notes with file, or other unique info about your files):

Process of starting and terminating with clients (may be needed to continue groups, for instance):

Calendar and schedule is maintained in this way:

Credit card processing information:

Current fees:

Other:

Other:

Other:

Initials _____

Please note that some or all of the following information may be left blank depending on the disposition of the practice or circumstances. *If your Professional Executor is joining or taking over the business, he or she will need this information. In most circumstances, all that is likely to be needed is to designate any details about your personal property that is in your office.*

Liabilities - Office Lease (location, term, contract, contacts):

Liabilities - Office Lease (as above, for a second location):

Liabilities - Additional Leases (furniture, equipment, etc.):

Liabilities - Other:

Assets - Subleases:

Assets - Real Property:

Assets - Personal Property (furniture, books, office decor, etc.):

Assets - Electronic Property (computer, printer, server, etc.):

Assets - Other:

Initials _____

Resources

1. Ethics in Psychotherapy and Counseling: A Practical Guide, 5th Edition by Kenneth S. Pope, Ph.D., ABPP & Melba J.T. Vasquez, Ph.D., ABPP, published by John Wiley. Copyright ©2016.

2. Ethical guidelines for the American Counseling Association are at this link: www.counseling.org/knowledge-center/ethics
(see sections A.2.b.; A.4.a.; B.6.i.; C.2.h.)

3. The American Association of Marriage and Family Therapist ethical guidelines are at this link: www.aamft.org/Legal_Ethics/Code_of_Ethics.aspx
(see sections 1.2; 1.11; 2.3; 2.5; 2.6)

4. The National Associates of Social Workers ethical guidelines are at this link: www.socialworkers.org/about/ethics/code-of-ethics/code-of-ethics-english
(see sections 1.03; 1.07(t); 1.08; 1.15; 1.17; 3.04)

5. The American Psychiatric Association published guidelines are at this link: www.psychiatry.org/psychiatrists/practice/ethics

The guidelines indicate that psychiatrists are expected to follow the American Medical Association guidelines for medical professionals, as well as the specifically annotated guidelines for psychiatrists.

6. The American Psychological Association's Ethical Principles of Psychologists and Code of Conduct is at this link: www.apa.org/ethics/code/index
(see sections 3.04; 3.10; 3.12; 6.02c)

7. The National Board for Certified Counselors Code of Ethics is at this link: www.nbcc.org/Assets/Ethics/NBCCCodeofEthics.pdf
(see directive 10)

8. The Code of Ethics for the National Association of Addiction Professionals is at this link: www.naadac.org/code-of-ethics
(see sections I-3e; II-28; III-44; IX-15)

9. The Code of Ethics of the American Mental Health Counselor Association is located at this link: www.amhca.org/publications/ethics
(see sections C.1.0; E.1.b)

10. The Ethics and Standards Guidelines published by the British Association for Counselling and Psychotherapy (BACP) is located at this link: www.bacp.co.uk/events-and-resources/ethics-and-standards/

11. A description of Business Associate Agreement provisions is available on the United States Health and Human Services website at this link: www.hhs.gov/hipaa/for-professionals/covered-entities/sample-business-associate-agreement-provisions/index.html

12. Link to the form to deactivate a National Provider Identifier (NPI): www.cms.gov/Medicare/CMS-Forms/CMS-Forms/downloads/cms10114.pdf

Note that the ethical guidelines and Codes of Ethics for various organizations are provided for reference, and are current as of the date this book was published. If you are in a country outside of the United States or the United Kingdom it is recommended that you review any ethical guidelines specific to your country and professional designation. In addition, clinicians may need to also review ethical guidelines or requirements based on state or local laws, and professional organizations.

Several common areas of ethical guidelines relate to creating and maintaining a professional will. The sections I referenced above relate to the list below, and if you need to verify guidelines yourself based on your location or professional designation, these may help you search for appropriate sections that pertain to you:

- Informed consent – part of informed consent can include being informed of what will happen in the event a clinician is unable to continue with a client, including who has their records;
- Reasonable precautions and avoiding harm – we are expected to take reasonable precautions to avoid harming a client;
- Having a specific plan for incapacitation, death, retirement or termination of practice;
- Access to records and records retention.

Table of Figures

Index

NPPES, 43

O

operations manual, 48

P

passwords, 29, 41, 44, 54

pdf, 30, 79

Personal Representative, 19, 24, 33, 41, 42

personnel file, 48

PHI, 6, 25, 56

photos, 12, 54

Power of Attorney, 25, 35

professional association, 15

professional designations, xviii

Professional Executor, xviii, 2, 3, 8, 9, 10, 11, 12, 13, 20, 21, 22, 23, 24, 25, 26, 27, 29, 32, 33, 35, 38, 40, 41, 42, 43, 45, 47, 48, 49, 50, 53, 54, 55, 57, 59

Professional Executor's, 13, 42

professional liability, 15, 49

professional organization, xi, 50

Professional Will Template, 30, 62

Protected Health Information, 56

R

record retention, 22, 56

records, xvii, xviii, 3, 5, 6, 19, 21, 40, 47, 48, 54, 56, 57, 80

referrals, 2, 11, 13

Retention of Records, 40

review, 12, 39, 49, 50, 53, 54, 56, 79

risk, 6, 9, 12, 21, 54

S

self-care, 55, 59

support group, 27

T

telehealth, 44

teletherapy, 44

U

update, xix, 24, 34, 50

W

witnesses, 36

About Cathy Wilson

Cathy Wilson, LPC, ACS, is the Director of LifePaths Counseling Center, a group of counselors practicing in Littleton, Colorado. She received her degree in Community Counseling from Regis University in Denver, and has been providing counseling services to individuals, couples and families for more than ten years. In 2012, she converted her individual practice to a group to both collaborate with other clinicians as well as be able to provide quality services to more people in the community. Cathy is an active member of several mental health communities such as local consultation groups and the American Counseling Association; and she is also an Approved Clinical Supervisor. In 2018, she began conducting workshops on creating your professional will for mental health practitioners, and has been able to help many colleagues gain the peace of mind of completing this important task. You can find more information about her and about LifePaths at www.lifepathscounseling.com, and more about her future work related to professional wills at www.onelastact.net.

About Julie Jacobs

Julie Jacobs is a licensed psychologist and attorney who practices in the area of mental health provider law. Julie received her Psy.D. in Clinical Psychology from the Georgia School of Professional Psychology and her J.D. from the University of Colorado Law School. Prior to attending law school, Julie practiced for 12 years as a clinical psychologist in a variety of settings, including private practice and as a Captain in the United States Air Force. Julie has established a small practice in Colorado focused on optimizing the work of mental health providers through consultations on legal, ethical, and risk management issues. She also works as a Risk Management Consultant for The Trust, providing ethics and risk management consultations to psychologists insured through The Trust Sponsored Professional Liability Insurance Program as well as presenting workshops and other educational content related to psychology on behalf of The Trust. In addition, Julie serves as the Chair of the Legislative Committee for the Colorado Psychological Association, focusing on legislative advocacy related to mental health providers.

www.ingramcontent.com/pod-product-compliance
Lightning Source LLC
Chambersburg PA
CBHW080546090426
42734CB00016B/3216